Plun

A Catholic Bathroom Book

PracticalPurity.com

Plunging Pornography: A Catholic Bathroom Book

Cincinnati, Ohio
PracticalPurity.com

Books are available in quantity for promotional or premium use. For information on discounts and terms, please visit our website: PracticalPurity.com.

The author recognizes the need for further scientific research on the neurological and psychological effects of Internet pornography use. The views and opinions expressed by the author are not intended to be a substitute for professional, medical or psychological advice.

Illustrations by Night Owl Animation Studio Los Angeles, CA

ISBN 978-0-692-76049-9
Printed in PRC

INTEGRITY RESTORED

Integrity Restored is a not for profit ministry of Stewardship: A Mission of Faith [a 501(c)(3) organization]. Integrity Restored is proud of our partnership with Plunging Pornography in support of our efforts to help parents and their teens. The proceeds from this book will support Integrity Restored's ongoing efforts in this mission.

Contents

Why Plunge Pornography from Your Life

Section 1: Porn...Silent, but Deadly........ 5
(The porn industry & its popularity)

Section 2: The Science of Smut........ 13
(How porn harms the user)

Section 3: Pain Behind the Pictures........ 29
(How porn harms other people)

How to Plunge Pornography from Your Life

Section 4: Theology of the Body on the Potty........ 35
(The true purpose of sexuality)

Section 5: Make the Love P.A.C.T. to Defeat Porn........ 43
(The practical steps to pursue purity)

Resources

Potent Potty Prayers........ 66
(Purity prayers listed out for you)

Parent Page........ 71
(Conversation starters for parents)

Acknowledgements........ 73

References........ 74

An Invitation...

Paramedic school taught me a lot of things. I learned how to poke people with needles, shock human hearts with electricity, and drill into bones.

Yes...I said DRILL INTO HUMAN BONES. The technical term for this is "Intraosseous Infusion." In order to save someone's life, you literally have to take a power-drill to their shinbone. Pretty crazy, right?

When I started working at the fire department, I put off the opportunity to train on the bone-drill. I figured the chances of me actually using it were slim, so why rush the training? BIG MISTAKE.

My ambulance was called to a horrific accident. Motorists frantically led us to a teenager who had been hit by a car. The kid was in bad shape, so we loaded them into the ambulance and got to work. My partner yelled for me to do an Intraosseous Infusion.

Every muscle in my body froze with fear as I quickly realized...I DIDN'T TRAIN FOR THIS.

My heart dropped at the thought of a person dying due to my lack of training. Thankfully, my partner switched places with me, and he did the bone-drilling.

Plunging Pornography

We successfully got the patient to the hospital in time.

Training is important.

Okay… you may never have to do an emergency bone-drilling in your life, but there is one thing you will have to do. LOVE. God commands us to love. And if it's real love, it will require you to sacrifice your selfish desires for the sake of someone else's benefit. Are you prepared to sacrifice for the sake of love? I know I wasn't.

You see, for most of my life, I had a dirty little secret. I was a porn user. And my hidden porn habit almost took the best part of my life… my ability to love. I didn't even realize the extent of the damage until after I was married. I relived that "bone-drill moment" every time love required me to sacrifice my selfishness. My heart would drop as the reality slapped me in the face:

I didn't know how to love my wife…I DIDN'T TRAIN FOR THIS.

Are you training to be a lover or a user? Every day of your life is filled with training opportunities, and porn is the ultimate training tool for users. I know you've probably seen porn, but I didn't come here to judge you. I came here with an invitation for something better than porn. An invitation to freedom.

The decision is yours to make:

Option #1: Stop reading this book and settle for the fake love offered by pornography.

Or

Option #2: Continue reading in search of the freedom to love.

Good choice.

If you've fallen into a habit of using porn, don't despair. There is a way out. By using the information in this book, you'll discover a type of freedom that few find. The freedom to love. R-e-a-l-l-y love. As someone who fought for years to escape a porn addiction, I can honestly tell you a porn-free life is worth the fight.

> **"Freedom exists for the sake of love."[B]**
> **-St. Pope John Paul II**

After you experience real love, you will want to rise to its demands. Love requires training in sacrifice, and the training starts now. Let's fight porn today, so you can have a chance at love tomorrow.

It's my heartfelt desire that you read this book and place it on the toilets of others who may be affected by the toxic plague of pornography. I'm praying for you.

"To love is to will the good of another" (CCC 1766)

Section 1:

PORN... SILENT, BUT DEADLY

"For we are the aroma of Christ to God among those who are being saved and among those who are perishing, to one a fragrance from death to death, to the other a fragrance from life to life."
2 Corinthians 2:15-16

Porn. Patent Pending...

"Pornography" comes from the Greek word *pornographos,* which means "writing about prostitutes." [1]

Porn has been around for a long time. A really long time. People have even found pornographic paintings from ancient civilizations; so, porn is nothing new. What is new? Our technology.

Porn has come a long way since the painted pottery of ancient Greece. It weaseled its way into the mainstream and exploded with the dawn of the Internet. There are now hardcore HD videos streaming online 24/7.

Here's how the Catholic Catechism defines pornography:

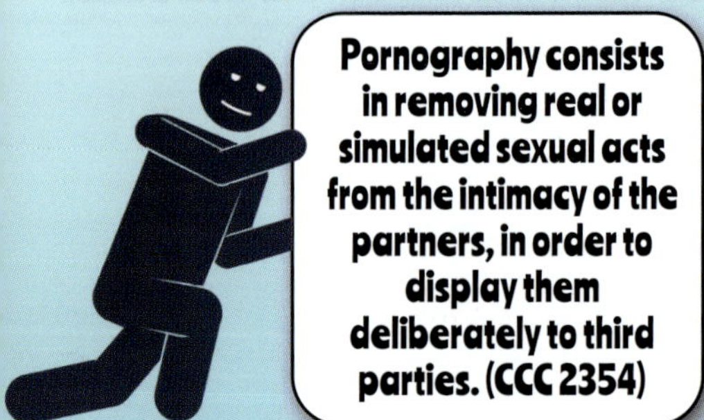

Porn can take the form of videos, images, writings, drawings, audio recordings, live performances, video games, etc...

Plunging Pornography

Massive exposure when there's no enclosure...

Porn has never been more accessible than now.

It's like we're living in the Wild West of Internet pornography...no one is safe. Porn can potentially pop up on every device we own. If it has an Internet connection, it has a porn connection.

Even Grandma has to watch her back because the porn monster may be lurking behind every corner. Playing video games...PORN VIDEOS! Driving in the car...PORN BILLBOARDS! Grocery shopping... PORN MAGAZINES! Visiting the library... INTERNET PORN!

Our ancestors could have gone their entire lives without seeing a single pornographic image, but now we are assaulted by porn imagery everywhere we turn.

Some have labeled this time period as the "largest unregulated social experiment in human history."[5]

YOU are a test subject in a worldwide porn experiment whether you've seen porn or not.

Porn Traps

Porn is looking for you. Seriously. Porn companies have a history of using sneaky techniques to sink their hooks into future customers. Here are a few traps for which they're known:

The Domain Name Snatch Game:
Pornographers buy website names in an effort to redirect people to porn sites. During history class, my fellow 7th grade classmates and I were exposed to porn after we innocently typed "Whitehouse.com" into the browser. We didn't know the actual domain name for the White House is "Whitehouse.gov." An Internet entrepreneur named Dan Parisi purchased the "Whitehouse.com" name and put porn on it.

Mr. Parisi received complaints from angry parents and White House staff members, but he still kept the site up for several years. He finally shut the site down after he became a father. [6]

If a domain name isn't renewed, porn companies immediately buy them. This happened to a Scout Troop's website in Virginia. When they forgot to pay for their site's subscription, a porn company snatched it up and transformed the scout site into a smut site. Imagine how shocked the parents were when they logged onto the website!

The owner of "WhiteHouse.com" received a letter from the White House demanding its removal.

Popcorn Porn:
Pornographers are known for using software that forces new sites to "pop up" when you try to exit a porn site. Clicking the "X" makes more X-rated content appear.

Sleazy Social Media:
Pornographers take full advantage of social media. They send friend requests to unsuspecting people in an effort to redirect them to their porn sites.

New porn traps are being set every minute. Don't get snared!

Porn Propaganda

Pornographers desperately try to take the punch out of viewing porn by labeling it "normal behavior."

One porn site launched a marketing campaign with the slogan, "*All You Need Is Hand,*" which is a spin-off of the old Beetles song, "*All You Need Is Love.*" They posted billboards in New York City's Times Square and even hired a choir to sing the porn slogan!

Plunging Pornography

Some porn companies try to portray themselves as "honorable" businesses. One site attempted to justify porn by giving money to breast cancer, testicular cancer, and environmental charities in exchange for video clicks on their site.

The same site held a $25,000.00 scholarship competition with the description:

"We work hard to help make millions of people feel happy every single day. In turn, we would like to help support the recipient of the [porn company] Scholarship to realize their goal of doing the same!" [7]

The stigma continues to fade as porn is pumped into our homes by the mainstream media. St. John Paul the Great said, *"Young people are threatened... by the evil use of advertising techniques that stimulate the natural inclination to avoid hard work by promising the immediate satisfaction of every desire."*[8]

Lust is easy. Love is not. Despite the culture's attempts to normalize pornography, we have to remember the truth: ***Sex is normal, but watching actors have sex on camera is not.***

The Legality of Lust...

Is distributing porn illegal? Umm…technically.

"Hardcore" porn isn't necessarily considered free speech under the First Amendment of the Constitution, but this hasn't stopped pornographers. Most porn companies find creative ways around these restrictions.[10]

The more questions I ask about porn's legality, the more confused I get. There doesn't seem to be a clear-cut answer.

The height of my confusion happened when I spoke with public library workers. They sheepishly admitted that people are allowed to access porn with public library computers. That means our tax dollars support porn habits!

God bless America… land of publicly-funded porn?

Porn's legality has been overshadowed by a mentality of morality impartiality. In other words…it's confusing.

Keep Reading!

Section 2:

The Science of Smut

"And they perverted their minds and turned away their eyes from looking to Heaven or remembering righteous judgements. Both were overwhelmed with passion"
Daniel 13:9-10

The Porn Pill

Porn is a drug.

I describe it as *cocaine snorted through the eyeballs*. Porn works the same way other drugs do. It enters the body and tricks it into releasing chemicals. Neural scientist, Dr. William M. Struthers, described how porn enters the brain:

"It comes in through the retina, goes through the thalamus, then projects up to the visual cortex, goes through the association cortex and the anterior cingulate, which then projects down to the insular cortex, the mirror neuron system, and the basal ganglia, thalamus and the hypothalamus. This is the sexual arousal center, that interstitial nucleus of the anterior hypothalamus sends projections down to the ventral tegmental area, which then releases dopamine." [11]

With the help of porn, chemicals like dopamine, norepinephrine, serotonin, oxytocin, and vasopressin go on a joyride through the neural pathways of the brain. Are these chemicals natural? Of course, but porn unnaturally releases them.

When its chemicals are abused, the brain gets confused.

Obsene Dopamine

Ah, dopamine…the craving chemical. It's the stuff that tells your brain, "I want that so let's go get it!"

Consider the smut cycle that happens when Internet porn artificially triggers the release of dopamine:

Step 1: John uses porn.

Step 2: John's brain releases a massive amount of dopamine.

Step 3: John's brain becomes physically re-wired due to his brain's massive dopamine dump.

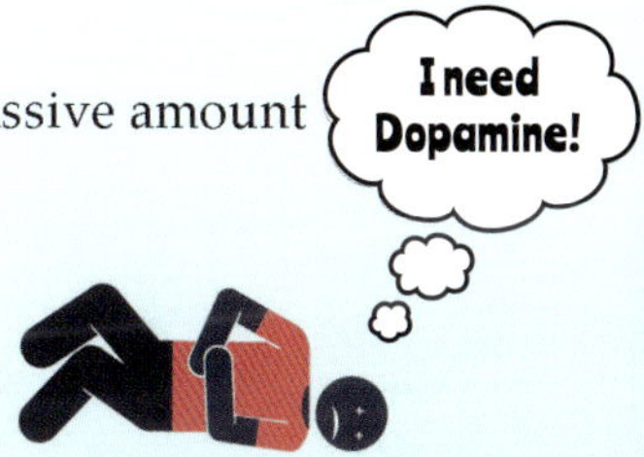

Step 4: John's brain is now programmed to CRAVE porn.

Step 5: John visits the Internet for more porn.

The porn habit recipe only requires a few ingredients...

(1) Endless supply of Internet porn
(1) Easily trainable brain
(1) Large amount of unsupervised free time

Mix the ingredients together and VOILA! You've created a genuine porn habit. The habit is easy to create, but hard to escape.

Linkage to Shrinkage?

Porn treats the brain like a screaming baby treats a TV remote. IT CHAOTICALLY HITS EVERY BUTTON UNTIL ALL THE TV SETTINGS ARE SCRAMBLED.

Plunging Pornography

Porn overwhelms the brain's reward circuitry, which messes with the motivation settings. It may even shrink the size of the user's brain.

Did you catch that? PORN. MAY. CAUSE. SHRINKAGE. OF. THE. BRAIN.

Scientists discovered that the longer a man uses porn, the less "Grey matter" he has in the reward section of his brain. Grey matter matters! [12]

Messed up Reward Circuits = Messed up Motivations.

A compulsive porn user might eventually choose porn over important things like homework, exercise, or even friends. One guy told me he continually chose porn over sleep! He would regularly stay awake watching porn into the early morning hours, even when he knew he had to wake up early for school. Everything else became dull compared to the pornographic pixels.

Porn eventually downsizes the dopamine delivery sensitivity, and the person will need new and extreme types of porn to achieve the same level of "high."

A human chasing a hormone is like a dog chasing its tail. It's pointless and endless.

Porn Kills the Will

I wasn't a very good decision maker during my teenage years. It's a miracle I'm still alive.

My parents had a creek running through their backyard called "Muddy Creek." A better name for it would've been "Fecal Creek" because the water was filled with garbage, and it smelled like fecal matter.

During rain storms, the once calm and smelly creek would transform into a ferocious whitewater river. The garbage-filled rapids would violently beat against the jagged rocks. Needless to say, no one would ever want to swim in this water.

Except one time.

My friends and I thought it might be fun to jump in and face the rancid rapids. So, we dove into the water. We didn't stop to think about safety; we just went for it!

Long story short, one of my friends almost drowned. He had to go to the hospital to get treated for the parasitic infection he contracted while nearly drowning in the poop water. He also received a week of diarrhea as an added "parting gift." (My friends and I all received this gift as well.)

Bad Decisions = Bad Results.

Plunging Pornography

We've all made poor decisions, but porn users are setting themselves up to be bad decision makers. Porn can literally hold a conscience captive.

The area of your brain responsible for willpower is called the prefrontal cortex. It's in charge of controlling your impulses and weighing the costs and benefits of your actions.

Brain scans have shown that this area of the brain is smaller in regular porn users. So, using porn may literally shrink the brain, wear away the willpower, and kill the conscience. [13]

You can see the weakened willpower of porn users in news headlines like "National spokesperson loses job due to porn habit!" and "Man crashes car and dies while watching porn on his phone!"

"Conscience is a judgment of reason whereby the human person recognizes the moral quality of a concrete act that he is going to perform, is in the process of performing, or has already completed." (CCC 1778)

It seems crazy to risk your life for an image on a screen, but you have to understand what these people were up against. They were fighting a battle with a weakened spirit and a damaged brain.

Porn can do more than damage a person's character; it can damage their chemistry.

Permanent Pornography

My friend suffered from Post Traumatic Stress Disorder (PTSD) after returning home from his military deployment. He would regularly relive the horrific war images in his head. The images had been burned into his memory.

Military veterans can suffer from war-related PTSD. Porn veterans can suffer from porn-related PTSD.

When someone views pornography, the chemical *norepinephrine* is released. It chemically burns the porn image into the memory, similar to what happens when soldiers see graphic war scenes. [14]

I stumbled upon pornography in the 1st grade and that image stuck with me for nearly 20 years, thanks to this chemical scarring.

People often carry these scars with them into future relationships, which means, porn can ruin your marriage before you even meet your spouse.

Married to a Movie Screen?

Randy, a retired porn star, was asked about all the women he "performed with" throughout his career. He said he didn't have sex with any of the women; he just used their bodies to masturbate. [15]

Plunging Pornography

That sounds gross, but it's true. Porn ruins sexual intimacy.

Many porn users end up treating their spouse like a movie screen instead of a person. Porn pries away the humanity of the user's spouse and turns them into a blank screen upon which their pornographic memories are projected. It robs you of the ability to see the value of the person, and if you downsize your spouse's dignity, you will downsize their identity. They'll be reduced to a warm body whose only *use* is pleasure.

When Bishop Fulton Sheen wrote his book, *Three to Get Married,* he didn't mean husband, wife, and porn. He meant husband, wife, and God. You deserve to be married to a person, not a movie screen.

Crashing the Sex Drive

As weird as the picture to the right is, that's exactly what happens with porn users.

Their brains become programmed to prefer pictures over people. The re-wiring can be so severe that the person becomes unable to sexually perform with their partner.

Scientists found that many porn users were unable to become aroused by their partner (a real person), but had no problem being aroused by porn (pictures on a screen). [16]

Not only does porn distort the true meaning of sex, it renders some people impotent, PHYSICALLY UNABLE TO HAVE SEX.

Porn crashes the sex drive.

Porn Clicks and Ugly Sticks

Clicking on porn is like metaphorically hitting your partner with an "ugly stick." Every click makes them less attractive.

Porn can't change a person's physical appearance, but it can alter your perception of attractiveness. Researchers found that men rated their wives or girlfriends as "less attractive" after one exposure to porn. [17]

You're ultimately faced with the decision:

Porn or my partner?

Sexual Tension Prevention

Why would God give us so much sexual tension and not expect us to need a RELEASE?

Trying to get rid of sexual tension by using porn is like trying to get rid of a bully by handing over your lunch money. You've just guaranteed that the tension, and the bully, will be back. It's a temporary fix that creates a permanent problem.

When someone views pornography (or even dwells on a pornographic thought) their body releases chemicals that ramp up their sexual anticipation. It's kind of like throwing lighter fluid on a fire. [18]

Remember, every time you point the finger at someone else, three of your own fingers point right back at you. So if you're suffering from severe sexual tension, ask yourself if your actions are the cause.

You can usually turn the tension off by turning the pornography off.

Lust or Combust?

What happens to the millions of sperm cells if they're not released from the body via masturbation?

Do they hopelessly wander about the body with

their hands in their pockets while kicking cans?

Hmm…that seems unlikely.

Sperm are specialized cells. And just like other cells in the body, they can grow old. When cells exceed their "shelf-life," the body breaks them down and recycles them. If an old sperm isn't released from the body, it will likely get recycled, too. If a man's body needs to release any excess sperm it may do so in a perfectly natural way called a *nocturnal emission* or *wet dream.*

So, a person won't die from lack of "release."

Porn Infused Sexual Cues

Porn trains the brain to spring into "porn mode" at the drop of a hat.

Remember Ivan Pavlov's scientific experiments with dogs? He trained dogs to associate food with the sound of a ringing bell. After some conditioning, the dogs automatically drooled every time Pavlov rang the bell.

In the same way Pavlov conditioned dogs to associate non-food items with food, porn can train the brain to associate non-sexual things with sex.

A pornified brain gets confused with sexual cues which leads to a chain reaction of attraction.

Plunging Pornography

Porn users have admitted to developing some seriously warped sexual attractions after viewing porn.

Clothing...
Some porn users say underwear, shoes, or other types of clothing have become sexual arousal triggers for them. [19]

Violence...
Porn is filled with violence. Nearly 90% of popular porn scenes contain acts of violence. And when violence becomes sexualized, the brain gets re-wired to interpret rape as *sexy*. [20]

In fact, some Internet porn is literally rape caught on camera. [21] Rapists have recorded their crimes, and uploaded the footage to the web. Some porn users have seen real rape recordings without even realizing it. [22]

Same sex...
Because of the porn user's need for novelty, heterosexual men may find themselves developing attractions to transgender or homosexual porn. Internet forums are filled with testimonies from heterosexual porn users who have become confused about their own sexual orientation. [23] Why? Because their brains have been re-wired by pornography. [24]

Many porn users said their altered attractions went back to normal after they completely cut porn out of their lives.[25]

The Scent of Lament

I remember the worst odor I have ever smelled in my life. It was the bedroom of a home I entered while responding to an emergency call. The smell was so bad that my fellow paramedics and I had to plug our nostrils.

I was amazed that someone could live in such nasty conditions! The person had become desensitized to the awful stench of animal waste that filled their home. Apparently, people can become desensitized to disgusting smells over time. This is due to a phenomenon called *Sensory Adaptation.*

A similar adaptation occurs with pornography users. You can become desensitized to the gross behavior seen in porn.

You may initially be disgusted by the sight of a woman being degraded, cursed at, and physically assaulted; however, you eventually grow numb to the repulsive sounds and imagery.

The longer a porn habit persists, the more likely a porn user will push the envelope. You start off viewing soft-core porn and eventually find yourself viewing disgustingly violent, hard-core videos. There's a drop in pleasure when there's no shock value. [26]

Desensitized porn viewers fuel commercialized rape.

Making a Molester

A fraternity was banned from Yale a few years ago for harassing women outside their dorms. They chanted, "NO MEANS YES! NO MEANS YES!"

Something had trained these young men to think of rape as "cool." Was it porn? Maybe. Porn and rape have a strong relationship. I would even go as far as saying porn is a rapist's best friend.

- **Porn makes rapists more accepted by society.** Studies show that porn users belittle rape as a criminal offense. [27]

- **Rapists love watching porn.** Nearly 90% of rapists regularly view porn and the majority of them admit to "acting out" the pornography they've seen. [28]

- **Porn helps rapists hone their skills.** The infamous serial rapist, Ted Bundy, admitted that porn was "central to the development of [his] vile behavior." [29]

•**Porn helps pedophiles manipulate their victims.** The FBI reports that pedophiles typically show porn to their victims as part of the grooming process. [30]

Internet pornography is like online "rape school" and unfortunately, every rapist is awarded a full scholarship.

Viewing = Doin

"Oh no!" "He broke his leg!"

The comments poured in as the injured Louisville basketball player cried out in pain. Thousands of fans winced and clutched their legs as the violent injury replayed on the screen.

Why did fans grab their own legs? It may be due to brain cells called mirror neurons.

With the help of mirror neurons, your brain secretly acts out the actions you see. As far as the brain is concerned, there's little difference between viewing and doing. [31]

That might explain why I still got an adrenaline rush during my high school football games despite being a bench-warmer. My brain got into the game while my body was standing on the sidelines.

Plunging Pornography

The same is true when someone watches porn. The user's brain behaves as though it is the actor in the porn scene. So, it's not too surprising when porn users begin reenacting the onscreen behaviors...their brains have already "practiced" the actions. [32]

It brings a whole new meaning to Jesus' words:

"You have heard that it was said, 'You shall not commit adultery.' But I say to you that every one who looks at a woman lustfully has already committed adultery with her in his heart." (Matthew 5:27-28)

Jesus knew about mirror neurons!

Section 3:

PAIN BEHIND The PICTURES

"There is no dignity when the human dimension is eliminated from the person. In short, the problem with pornography is not that it shows too much of the person, but that it shows far too little."

–St. John Paul II

Second-Hand Porn

My friend died from lung cancer even though he never smoked. He did, however, work at a place where *second-hand smoke* polluted the air. Porn, like tobacco, affects more people than just the person using it. Many people experience the effects of *second-hand porn* despite never using it themselves.

I remember speaking with a young man who tearfully explained to me the pain he felt from his dad's porn addiction.

He said, "*I couldn't even go in the computer room of my house anymore. I was bombarded with the horrible feeling that my dad used that computer to look at porn. So, I got a job at McDonald's and saved enough money to buy a new computer for my school work. I just couldn't bear the thought of using the computer that led to my parents' divorce.*"

Family, friends, and partners all suffer along with the porn user via social isolation, cheating, divorce, sexual abuse, and financial ruin. Many partners of porn users even admit to having lower self-esteem due to *second-hand porn.* [34]

Porn is an equal opportunity destroyer that damages the lives of users and non-users alike.

Internet Traffic Drives Sex Trafficking

Slavery has been outlawed for decades, but the American slave trade is still going strong.

Thousands of women and children are forced into sex slavery every day in America. A fifteen year-old girl was lured into a car while she was standing in the front yard of her suburban home in Arizona. She was locked in a dog cage by her kidnappers, who threatened to kill her family if she tried to escape. After being sexually assaulted by over 50 men, she was eventually rescued by police. This stuff really happens, and every time you click on porn you indirectly support it. [35]

The sex slavery business is booming because there is a demand for it. Why is there a high demand? PORN. Porn is the fuel that keeps the sex trafficking train moving down the track.

The average sex trafficking victim's age is thirteen years old. [36]

Men who purchase prostitutes (often sex slaves) are enslaved by their lustful desires.

Pray for Porn Stars

Isn't porn okay as long as the actors agreed to it?

As a paramedic, I've saved the lives of many drug-overdosed patients. Should I have let them die because they "chose" to get high?

It doesn't matter how a person gets into a dangerous situation. The only proper response to a person is love. Encouraging them to continue down a deadly path is the opposite of love.

The same is true for the people in the porn industry. It doesn't matter how that person got into porn, we shouldn't encourage their self-destructive behavior. I've heard porn users say, "I'm just doing my part to help this girl pay her bills!" That's like me saying, "I'm just helping this unconscious, drug-overdosed patient achieve a better 'high' by pumping more heroin into their veins!" If you use porn, you're *exploiting* the person, not *supporting* the person.

I scanned the fan mail from a young porn star's social media page. Many of her fans wrote that they "love her," but they don't really love her. They don't see the scars on her leg from the years of self-cutting. They don't see the remnants of the word "fat" carved into her leg with a razorblade. They don't know she was raped in high school and suffered from depression. They don't care about her life. They don't love her; they love pleasure.

If they really wanted to love her, they would stop *preying* on her and start *praying* for her.

Death or Divorce?

The most mentioned word in the comments section of porn sites is "love." [38]

A porny marriage is a thorny marriage.

Using porn greatly increases the chance of having a rocky marriage. In fact, porn contributes to OVER HALF of the Internet-related divorces in America. [39]

Marriage isn't an easy vocation where you have unlimited access to sexual satisfaction. Your selfishness must die or your relationship will die.

Love requires death to selfishness for the sake of dignity.

Porn requires death to dignity for the sake of selfishness.

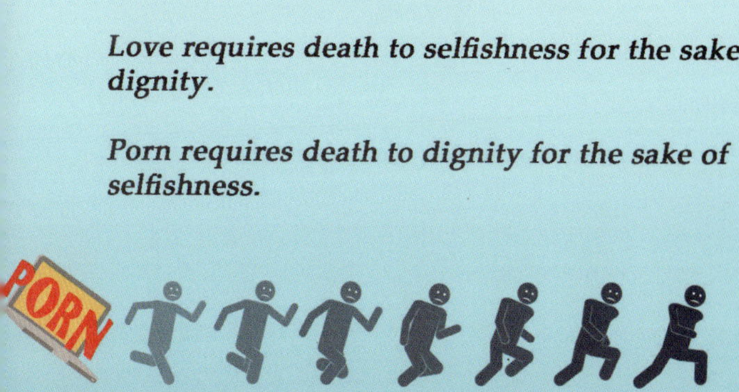

Keep Reading!

Section 4:

THEOLOGY OF THE BODY ON THE POTTY

"So God created man in his own image, in the image of God he created him; male and female he created them."
(Genesis 1:27)

Factory Reset

Every cell phone has a "factory reset" button. When pressed, it deletes all the extra stuff you've downloaded and restores the phone to the original settings.

It's time to hit your "factory reset" button so you can see God's original settings for your body.

It's easy to get discouraged when you see all the sexual dysfunction in the world, but Jesus promises that *"from the beginning it was not so."* (Matthew 19:8) Let's go back to what St. John Paul II called "Original Nakedness." It was the time when Adam and Eve perfectly understood and communicated the gift of their bodies. Understanding the true purpose of the body will require you to cut through the pornographic haze.

Why did God program *you* with sexual settings? Once you restore your settings back to the way they were *"in the beginning,"* you will see that sexuality and spirituality have a lot in common.

Dodging Desire

I became angry as I walked into the ocean. The powerful waves kept pelting me in the face. As I angrily fought against the water, I noticed a surfer gliding past me on his surfboard. I wished I could have harnessed the power of the waves like he did.

> **"Lust is disordered desire for or inordinate enjoyment of sexual pleasure. Sexual pleasure is morally disordered when sought for itself, isolated from its procreative and unitive purposes." (CCC 2351)**

Sexual desire is similar to an ocean wave. You can either harness its power or get pelted in the face with it. Attempting to repress it leads to misery.

Sexual desire is a gift from God; it should be there! With time, you can harness the power of your sexual desire like that surfer harnessed the power of the ocean waves. In order to harness its power, you must realize its purpose.

The Sexual Desire Purifier

You are created in the image and likeness of God, but who is God? An old man with a beard? Morgan Freeman?

No. God is a communion of persons. Although the Father, Son, and Holy Spirit are separate, They are one. It's impossible for the human brain to fully comprehend the mystery of the Trinity. It's like trying to lick your elbow…you can't do it!

Even though the Trinity is difficult to comprehend, God gave us sexual desire so we can understand a piece of His nature. So every time you experience strong sexual desire, remember its underlying meaning…**You are made for relationship with others because you are created in the image and likeness of God, who is relationship.** We are creatures created for communion, so we desire union with another human.

Sexual desire is fulfilled through vulnerability, not voyeurism. Porn users are left unfulfilled because temporary pleasure can never satisfy the infinite cravings of the heart. God alone satisfies. Seek communion with Him.

Love searches for the infinite, but porn is just an infinite search.

Crafted for Communion

This amazing call to Holy Communion is carved into our bodies. God is like an artist who hides His signature in His paintings. You are God's artwork and your body contains many signs that point to His communal nature.

Example 1: The mouth.

Why do humans kiss? Why doesn't the priest say to the wedding couple, "I now pronounce you husband and wife; you may high-five the bride!"?

Kisses are important.

The mouth is more than a food-hole. It is the very hole upon which we communicate with one another. It is the instrument upon which humans deeply connect with other humans through conversation. The mouth is also the very opening God chose to enter our bodies with the Eucharist.

Kisses are sacred. They point to the fact that you are made for communion.

Example 2: The bellybutton.

Ever wonder why you have a divot in your stomach? The bellybutton is more than a lint-catcher. It's a deeply theological piece of anatomy…even if you have an "out-ee."

This scar serves as a reminder that a tube once came out of your abdomen and attached you to another human being: your mother.

Bellybuttons are a stamp from God. They show us that we began life with human communion and we are destined to have full communion with our Creator.

So, think of God the next time you are digging a hair ball out of your bellybutton!

Example 3: The genitals.

These sacred "puzzle pieces" are a profound revelation of God's communal nature. If we look past the "pornographic haze" put forth by the devil, we can see God's signature in the marital embrace. Marital sex is more than natural…it's a supernatural sign that points to God!

The Trinity is a selfless exchange of love which brings forth abundant life. In a similar way, the marital embrace is a selfless exchange of love which brings forth human life (babies).

Sex is the greatest sign of God's communal nature imprinted in our bodies. And because sex is such a great sign of God's image, the devil ferociously attempts to distort it.

Plunging Pornography

Pornography is Satan's desperate attempt to distort our understanding of God. So let's cut through the pornographic noise and see that marital sex points to God.

Crucifixion or Porn Addiction?

"Truly, truly, I say to you, unless a grain of wheat falls into the earth and dies, it remains alone; but if it dies, it bears much fruit." (John 12:24)

You have a choice to make…Porn addiction or crucifixion?

Staying in a porn habit is easy. Leaving a porn habit is difficult. It will hurt. It will require mental, physical, and spiritual fortitude. It will demand sacrifice. It will demand death! Death to pride. Death to selfishness. Death to old neural pathways.

Christ laid down His life out of love for you. You must lay down your life out of love for Him. If you do this, a glorious resurrection will follow. Your wounds will be glorified and you will be a new person capable of authentic love.

You can do this!

> **"I have been crucified with Christ; it is no longer I who live, but Christ who lives in me; and the life I now live in the flesh I live by faith in the Son of God, who loved me and gave himself for me."**
> **(Galatians 2:20)**

Plunging Pornography

The battle for sexual freedom is both spiritual and carnal. (It involves body and soul.) So, in addition to the devil, you're facing a brain that has likely formed different reward circuitry. Be patient with yourself as the new circuitry grows and the old pathways are starved out. Remember the words of St. John Paul II.

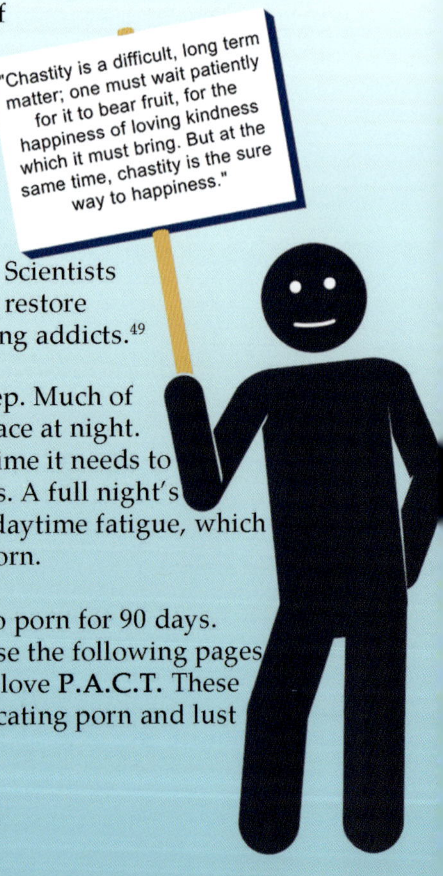

During the re-wiring and recovery time, make sure to:

Exercise. Regular exercise eases the re-wiring process. Scientists found that exercise helps to restore dopamine levels in recovering addicts.[49]

Sleep. Get a full night's sleep. Much of the brain re-wiring takes place at night. Sleep gives your brain the time it needs to erase the old porn pathways. A full night's sleep also helps you avoid daytime fatigue, which is usually a trigger to use porn.

Let's set an initial goal of no porn for 90 days. Take it one day at a time. Use the following pages to guide you in making the love **P.A.C.T.** These are essential steps for eradicating porn and lust from your life:

Section 5:

MAKE THE LOVE P.A.C.T. TO DEFEAT PORN

Prayer
Accountability
Communion
Triggers

Plunging Pornography

PRAYER

I fought to escape the grips of pornography for nearly a decade. My efforts began to gain traction the moment I began to develop a consistent prayer life. I remember the defining moment when the tide turned...

I had just lost a battle to pornography and was sitting in my bathroom feeling so disgusted with myself that I began to cry. That was the moment that I realized I was completely enslaved by pornography. I gave up. I admitted that I couldn't do this on my own. I needed help.

I finally pushed my massive ego aside and let God into my life. I prayed—really prayed—for the first time in years. I asked God to get me out of the porn cycle.

My wife was pregnant with our first child. I went into the newly decorated baby's room, laid face down on the floor, and tearfully begged God for the grace to be free from my addiction before my son was born.

That was my first encounter with God's infinite mercy and my last encounter with porn. Please understand, it wasn't as easy as *praying the porn away*. However, prayer brought about the graces I needed to help me take the necessary steps in the battle for freedom.

God is patiently waiting for you. Let Him in. After allowing God into my life I have little desire to return to the slavery of my past sins. I am free. You deserve freedom as well, and I firmly believe that freedom from sexual sin IS NOT POSSIBLE WITHOUT A SOLID PRAYER LIFE.

Here are my 7 prayer suggestions:

 # 1 Fasting:
Why is fasting important? Well, Jesus fasted for 40 days in the desert. If He did it, then it must be important. In fact, when the apostles were unable to expel a demon from a boy, Jesus told them, *"This kind cannot be driven out by anything but prayer and fasting."* (Mark 9:29) Porn is a serious problem that REQUIRES fasting.

Fasting accompanies prayer like protein powder accompanies bodybuilding. Pumping iron without protein is okay, but it will take much longer to achieve body builder-sized muscles.

The same is true for our spiritual workouts. Many of

us walk around with wimpy souls in need of some *prayer protein*. So give fasting a try, and I guarantee you will make some serious spiritual gains.

You don't have to fast only from food. You can fast from many things like TVs, phones, computers, etc. Temporarily sacrifice something good and offer it up as prayer for yourself and others. By training yourself to sacrifice little pleasures, you will be able to sacrifice big pleasures when love demands it…AND LOVE WILL DEMAND SACRIFICE.

Every day you unknowingly train yourself to be a *lover* or a *user*. Love will inevitably come pounding on your door demanding self-denial for your beloved. Are you prepared to participate in the depths of authentic sacrificial love, or will you be left fluttering on the surface with the countless others who think superficial love is as good as it gets?

Let me let you in on a little secret… The treasure is found in the depths. Don't be afraid to deny pleasure for the sake of love because the love of pleasure can ruin the pleasure of love.

Include some fasting into your prayer life because prayer and fasting go together like... peanut butter and jelly, milk and cereal, ketchup and French fries…I think you get the idea.

 # 2 The Rosary:
The rosary is not just a therapy tool for old ladies with arthritis; it's a powerful spiritual weapon!

One of America's most renowned exorcists, Father Gary Thomas, was interviewed about demons. He affirmed the power of Mary's intercession during exorcisms. He said the prayers to Mary are sometimes more powerful than the exorcism rite itself. The rosary is a powerful spiritual weapon. [41]

Bishop Oliver Dashe Doeme, a bishop from a terrorist-infested region of Nigeria, recalled a vision he had a few years ago while praying before the Blessed Sacrament in his chapel. Jesus appeared in the vision and handed him a sword to defeat the terrorists. When the bishop was handed the sword, it turned into a rosary. [42]

I carry a metal rosary ring in my pocket at all times. Some refer to this type of rosary as a "brass knuckles rosary" because it looks like it could double as a self-defense weapon. My friend, a military veteran, took this concept a step further by having his rosary made out of bullet shell casings. The rosary is a powerful spiritual weapon and we must never forget it. Is it a coincidence that there are ten beads in a decade

of the rosary and ten letters in the words "P-O-R-N-W-E-A-P-O-N"? I think not. My recovery from pornography was stagnant until I utilized the powerful intercession of Mary. Pray the rosary!

If the rosary seems like too much, start off slow. Remember, prayer and weightlifting are similar. You don't begin by lifting huge amounts of weight. You gradually work your way up. The same is true with prayer. You will gradually build stronger prayer muscles with time.

> **"Give me an army saying the Rosary and I will conquer the world."**
>
> **-Blessed Pope Pius IX**

If you're a rosary beginner, many saints recommend starting with three Hail Mary's in the morning and three Hail Mary's at night. This is powerful because there is one prayer to honor each Person of the Trinity.

Which way to the chapel?

 # 3 The Mass:

The Mass is an amazing opportunity to witness and participate in Christ's saving sacrifice.

God literally gives us his flesh and blood in the Eucharist. Take advantage of this amazing gift and the abundant grace it brings.

The Mass is also a time to bring our prayer intentions to the foot of the cross. Go to Mass, worthily

> **"The Holy Eucharist, which is the Body of Christ, when worthily received, does diminish the uprisings of concupiscence."[43]**
>
> **-Bishop Fulton Sheen**

receive the Eucharist, and offer your prayers to all those struggling with the sin of pornography.

 # 4 The Chaplet of Divine Mercy:
This prayer is derived from the diary of St. Faustina, which contains her personal encounters with Jesus. Here is an excerpt of what Jesus said to St. Faustina during a vision:

"My Heart overflows with great mercy for souls, and especially for poor sinners. If only they could understand that I am the best of Fathers to them and that it is for them that the Blood and Water flowed from My Heart as from a fount overflowing with mercy. For them I dwell in the tabernacle as King of Mercy. I desire to bestow My graces upon souls, but they do not want to accept them." [44]

God is waiting to give you the grace to be a saint. All you have to do is ask!

If the Chaplet of Divine Mercy prayer seems too long, start by saying the phrase, "Jesus, I trust in You," three times every day at 3:00PM, which is the hour that our Lord died on the cross. Even if you don't fully trust in Him yet, say it anyway with the added petition of asking God for the grace to trust in Him.

 # 5 The Intercession of the Saints:
Asking a saint to intercede for you is like hiring sexual purity security. Because the saints are united with

God in Heaven, their prayers are more closely united with Him as well. Take advantage of their powerful intercession. Here are some saints to whom I regularly ask for prayers:

St. Maria Goretti
She was an eleven-year-old Italian girl murdered by a man who attempted to rape her. The killer, who stabbed Maria fourteen times, later had a massive change of heart and converted to Catholicism. Guess who helped him convert. St. Maria Goretti!

St. Maria interceded from heaven and spoke to him in a dream. Ask her to pray for the conversion of *your* heart.

St. Vitalis of Gaza
He was a monk who became a saint by using what little money he had to purchase prostitutes. He used his "purchased time" to preach to the prostitutes about their dignity. Many women left lives of prostitution and found God with the help of St. Vitalis.

Ask him to pray that *you* can see the dignity of every woman.

St. John Paul II
He survived multiple assassination attempts during his papacy and lived a heroic life of virtue. He also spoke with a brilliant understanding of love, sexuality, and the human person. Ask him to pray for *your* greater understanding of love.

St. Maximilian Kolbe
He was a priest who voluntarily died in place of a stranger while imprisoned in a German death camp during World War II. He is the patron saint of the imprisoned and addicted. Ask him to pray for *your* freedom from the slavery of lust.

It can be difficult to ask for help, especially when it comes to our desires, but remember the words of Jesus: *"Ask, and it will be given to you; seek, and you will find; knock and it will be opened to you. For every one who asks receives, and he who seeks finds, and to him who knocks it will be opened."* (Matthew 7:7-8)

 # 6 Silence:
God likes to whisper. So, if you want to hear the voice of God, you MUST silence your heart and mind.

Fight for silence.

One can easily get used to the noisiness of our world where the music is always playing, the TV is always on, and the phone is always ringing. I think our society has become uncomfortable with silence. Every moment is filled with noise.

Turn it off and experience the sound of silence. Just think, even non-religious people observe a moment of silence after a death or tragedy. Why? Because the silence is where God speaks and EVERYONE is searching for God. Seek Him in the silence.

Plunging Pornography

Make an effort to quiet your heart and mind during prayer. My favorite place to sit in silence is in front of the Blessed Sacrament at church. Go, sit, and be transformed.

Try sitting in silence and saying "Je" as you inhale and "sus" as you exhale.

#7 The Scriptures

If you ever get discouraged that you can't hear the voice of God during prayer don't worry. God is there.

An easier way to hear God's voice is by reading the Bible. God speaks to us directly through the scriptures. Read the Gospels (Matthew, Mark, Luke, and John) and He will likely put a word or phrase on your heart that speaks directly to you.

Don't let the Bible be the old dusty book that sits on the top shelf of the closet. Open it up! If you have a cell phone, you have a bible. There are apps that have the Church's daily readings. Some of the apps even read them to you.

The same readings are read at every Catholic Church around the world. Talk about "universal!"
There are literally no barriers between you and the Bible.

Download a Catholic Bible app or log onto usccb.org and read the Bible. God is waiting to communicate with you through His Word.

ACCOUNTABILITY

In 2003, Aron Ralston set out for a day of adventure in the remote canyons of Utah. While climbing, he accidentally dislodged an 800-pound boulder, which pinned his right arm against the canyon wall. He was trapped in the middle of nowhere.

His echoing cries for help were a useless reminder of his complete isolation. He was absolutely alone. After five days with no help, Aron was forced to break the bones in his wrist, cut his arm off with a dull pocketknife, repel down a 60-foot cliff, and hike seven miles to a rescue helicopter.

The results would have been radically different if Aron had just brought a friend with him. His 127-hour struggle for survival would have been reduced to a 3-hour rescue operation.

"And though a man might prevail against one who is alone, two will withstand him. A threefold cord is not quickly broken." (Ecclesiastes 4:12)

Aron's biggest mistake was hiking alone. Don't make the same mistake when striving for sexual purity. Tell someone about your struggle with porn. If your too nervous to tell a human, then start by telling your dog. Then tell a trusted friend. Gradually work your way up to telling your parents. I know it's scary, but hidden wounds cannot be healed.

Plunging Pornography

1) Be accountable to yourself:
St. Paul is clear with his instructions:

"But immorality and all impurity or covetousness must not even be named among you, as is fitting among saints. Let there be no filthiness, nor silly talk, nor levity, which are not fitting; but instead let there be thanksgiving." (Ephesians 5:3-4)

Destroy all access to porn. Get rid of anything that resembles pornography. Trash all the sleazy movies, pictures, and websites. Un-follow any shady social media friends that have provocative posts.

The path to purity starts by being honest with yourself. You are called to greatness, and you can't achieve greatness with pornography in your life.

2) Be accountable to others:
Having a human support system greatly increases your chances of escaping the porn trap. Find someone that you can call when you are tempted to use porn. Call them every time you're tempted.

"Therefore confess your sins to one another, and pray for one another, that you may be healed." (James 5:16)

Try to find an accountability partner who has the time to meet with you on a regular basis. Meet with them to share your victories and setbacks. Many priests would love to be your spiritual director and accountability partner. Just ask them.

Don't forget to filter. A porn addict surfing the Internet without a filter is like a drug addict lighting a crack pipe and placing it on the coffee table as a "decoration." It's risky business.

I get it; filters can sometimes be a little overprotective. That's why I recommend using accountability software for your computer, tablet, and cell phone. These programs work by sending your Internet or app history to an accountability partner of your choosing. *Covenant Eyes®* makes a reliable and inexpensive accountability software for phones and computers.

Don't count-out counseling. You may want to talk to a counselor. Yeah, I know...who would do that, right? Counseling can be a great tool for those who struggle with pornography. Maybe there is a deeper issue that has led to a person's use of pornography as a coping mechanism. The person who seeks counseling isn't weird. In fact, many people seek counseling at one point in their lives. I'm not ashamed to admit that I have sought after counseling and you shouldn't be either. Shame can be a tool from the devil to prevent you from finding healing.

Get more info on counseling and a free Covenant Eyes trial code at PracticalPurity.com

3) Be accountable to God:
Accidentally farting in public. Wetting the bed at a slumber party. Walking around with toilet paper

stuck to your shoe.

It's hard to think of anything more embarrassing than confessing the sin of pornography and masturbation to a priest. Confession can be scary. What if a priest tells his buddies all about your sins?

If he tells anyone your sins he gets kicked out of the Church. So don't worry, confession is a safe place for healing. In fact, priests are willing to go to jail before breaking the seal of the confessional.

I avoided going to confession for almost 9 years. But after I went, the heavy burden of my sins was lifted. You deserve to be forgiven for your sins. God is waiting to take the weight from you. Don't be afraid to give it to Him. And if you forget how to go to confession, just tell the priest. He will literally walk you through it step by step when you get there.

"And when He had said this, He breathed on them, and said to them, 'Receive the Holy Spirit. If you forgive the sins of any, they are forgiven; if you retain the sins of any, they are retained.'" (John 20:22-23)

Because sexual sins are sins of weakness, Satan will pour on the pride after you fall. Don't let it get to you. Go to confession and be forgiven for your sins. Many people end up bringing the same sins to confession every time they go. Don't be ashamed to confess the same sin many times.

Stop *stressing* and start *confessing*. An abundance of Sacramental Grace is waiting for you!

COMMUNION

Before joining a street gang, prospective members must undergo an extreme initiation ritual. Some rituals include being dowsed in urine and feces, being savagely beaten by fellow gang members, or even being forced to drink human blood.

Why would someone put themselves through such a dangerous and humiliating ordeal? Because human beings are hard-wired for intimacy, and when the relational requirement isn't met, a suffering person will go to extremes to get it. Some people join gangs, some people visit prostitutes, and some view pornography.

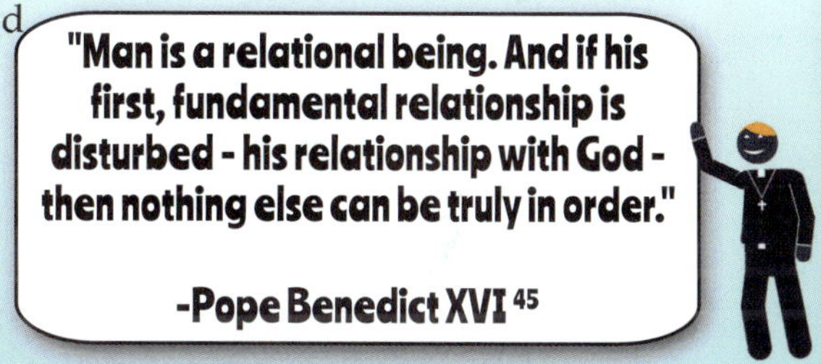

Pornography offers intensity, not intimacy. To get real intimacy you have to flip yourself inside out and share your feelings with someone. How many times have you hidden your feelings from a loved one? Interestingly enough, some of the most intimate moments in my life involved conversations with friends and family. *Satisfying intimacy* doesn't require *sexual intercourse.*

Intimacy is about sharing the most vulnerable areas of your heart. Pornography only touches the shallowest part of the person...the flesh. It offers an illusion of intimacy because the naked participants appear vulnerable, but in reality, their ability to be vulnerable has retreated into their vaulted hearts.

Porn, coupled with masturbation, doesn't satisfy the need for intimacy any more than chewing plastic while watching the cooking channel satisfies hunger. Porn points to our loneliness and intensifies the desire for intimacy.

> **"When you have sought the company of a sensual satisfaction, what loneliness afterward!"**
> **-St. Josemaria Escriva**

If you are really looking for satisfaction, you should pursue a loving relationship with Jesus. He is the one who truly satisfies our longing. He was pretty clear when He said, "*Every one who drinks of this water will thirst again, but whoever drinks of the water that I shall give him will never thirst; the water that I shall give him will become in him a spring of water welling up to eternal life.*" (John 4:13-14)

After someone falls to the sin of pornography the curtain is lifted. They realize they have been duped and their search for intimacy was in vain.

Plunging Pornography

Stop searching for the infinite love of God in the temporary pleasure of pornography.

TRIGGERS

> **"And if your hand causes you to sin, cut it off; it is better for you to enter life maimed than with two hands to go to hell, to the unquenchable fire."**
>
> **(Mark 9:43)**

In 2003, a man was sentenced to 6 months in prison for keeping a pet in his tiny New York City apartment. That might seem like a harsh punishment until you hear that his "pet" was actually a 500 lb. Bengal Tiger! The tiger was tame for a while, but its wild instincts eventually took over and it viciously attacked its owner. The owner survived and the tiger was moved to a more suitable location.

Recovering from a porn habit can be tough. You might feel like a wild animal is living in your house, and you're one wrong move away from triggering a brutal attack. Don't despair.

"God is faithful, and He will not let you be tempted beyond your strength, but with the temptation will also provide the way of escape, that you may be able to endure it." (1 Corinthians 10:13)

With time and perseverance, your temptations can shrink from a 500 pound tiger down to a 5 pound housecat. Even though it gets easier with time, you may feel overwhelmed and outgunned right now.

Plunging Pornography

If you're feeling defenseless against porn temptations, here are some tips to help you defeat the beast:

> **"Be sober, be watchful. Your adversary the devil prowls around like a roaring lion, seeking some one to devour." (1 Peter 5:8)**

Recognize the Trigger:
You will be tempted. Even our Lord, Jesus, faced temptations. (See Matthew 4:1-11). You must learn how to recognize them, and respond appropriately. Are you aware of the triggers that are capable of leading you into sexual sin? Triggers will be slightly different for each person, so it's important to know what your triggers are.

Triggers are sights, sounds, smells, feelings or activities that would typically send you down the path of porn *use*. They might be websites, TV shows, books, clothing, or even your mood.

Many people say they are more likely to fall into sin when they're depressed, tired, angry, lonely, or in another altered state of mind. I guess that's the reason Satan chose to tempt Jesus when He was hungry and tired after fasting in the desert for 40 days. Honestly analyze the last time you fell to the sin of porn. What were you doing right before you fell? That's one of your triggers.

Attack the Triggers:
Breaking a porn habit requires brain-retraining. You must kill the old brain pathways and grow new ones. This takes time and consistency.

When you are able to recognize your triggers, you can try to avoid them, but you will likely still encounter them. When a trigger approaches, you must attack! Resist the urge to be silent and passive. Jesus was never passive. Be like Jesus.

In the same way Jesus stopped people from defiling His Father's temple, you should stop anything that could defile the purity of your body, which is a temple of the Holy Spirit. (See 1 Corinthians 6:19)

"For the word of God is living and active, sharper than any two-edged sword" (Hebrews 4:12)

Verbally call out temptations. Literally say something out loud to label the temptation. When He was tempted by Satan, Jesus verbally responded by quoting Sacred Scripture. Be like Jesus. Quote Scripture when you're tempted.

When I am tempted by a visual trigger, I divert my eyes, and say the following sentence out loud: "*I am tempted to use that person but '**Blessed are the pure in heart, for they shall see God.**'*" (Matthew 5:8)

Say it out loud to yourself. I've found that pointing out the temptation and giving it to God works better than trying to repress it. Being attracted to someone is not a sin. So, if you're tempted to lust after a person, point out their attractiveness and give it to God.

Plunging Pornography

I understand temptations are a serious struggle for some people. Struggling with temptations can even be a form of suffering, which means there's great value in it. One major difference between saints and non-saints is how they respond to suffering. Temptations can be an opportunity to sin or an opportunity to pray. If you are suffering with intense temptations make sure your heart is in the right place.

Temptations don't have to point you to hell; they can point you to heaven. Struggling is good. It might be God's way of strengthening you and burning off the impurities.

When I deal with suffering I try to remind myself that God is with me. I carry a rosary with me and touch it whenever temptation arises and imagine the brutal images of Jesus' crucifixion. Jesus is suffering right alongside you. Let Him into your suffering.

"Blessed is the man who endures trial, for when he has stood the test he will receive the crown of life which God has promised to those who love him." (James 1:12)

When Impure Thoughts Pop Up...
Even the most holy of people cannot stop random impure thoughts from popping into their heads. Rest assured that you have not sinned if an uninvited, impure thought pops up out of nowhere. Here are some

practical tips to deal with these inopportune thoughts:

- **Fast forward the impure thought from its beginning to the consequences.**
- **Mentally visualize a red line crossing out the impure thought.** Some have also verbalized an annoying buzzer noise when the image is crossed out.
- **Imagine the impure thought as a picture and quickly visualize the image burning up.**
- **Touch a holy reminder like a blessed medal or a rosary.**
- **Bless yourself with Holy Water.**
- **Make the Sign of the Cross.**
- **Do some exercises like squats or push-ups.** This will divert your attention and blood flow to your muscles.
- **Visualize your funeral.** Although it may seem odd, visualizing death can force us to remember the weakness of the flesh.

"Peer into your grave often, looking at and touching, and smelling your own rotting corpse there, a week, no more, after your death. Remember this especially when you are troubled by the impulses of your flesh." [46]

-St. Josemaria Escriva

Plunging Pornography

Avoid autopilot. Many people fall into the sin of lust because they are bored. NEVER PUT YOURSELF IN THE SITUATION OF MINDLESS WEB SEARCHING. This might mean temporarily avoiding the Internet for a while.

Give the video games a rest. Video games may actually hinder your ability to re-wire your brain from the never-ending novelty of Internet porn. Turn the video games off. Go outside and implement a regular exercise routine.

Rest assured that temptations will decrease as your relationship with God increases. If you find success, be careful that you aren't tempted into pride. That is the Devil trying to regain a foothold in your life. Don't let him back in. You're less likely to stumble when you're sober and humble. *"For every one who exalts himself will be humbled, and he who humbles himself will be exalted."* (Luke 14:11)

> **"Temptations of the flesh become less as one gets closer to God, although the temptations to pride may increase."[47]**
> **-Bishop Fulton Sheen**

After You Fall...

What about the times you lose the battle to porn and lust?

Don't despair. God loves you. There is value in defeat. You now have a valuable learning opportunity

"God demands great purity of certain souls, and so He gives them a deeper knowledge of their own misery. Illuminated by light from on high, the soul can better know what pleases God and what does not."[48]
-St. Faustina

in front of you. Don't waste this time to grow in humility. Porn, unlike other sins such as greed, has a short "coming to your senses" period after you fall.

You're fighting a tough opponent that has distorted your desires. This is a great time to gain some clarity of mind. What were you really looking for during your battle with lust? Did it deliver? How do you feel now? What is one change you need to make to your battle plan?

Get up. Dust yourself off. You can do this.

"For a righteous man falls seven times, and rises again; but the wicked are overthrown by calamity."
(Proverbs 24:16)

Purity Prayers

The Rosary:
Begin with the sign of the cross:
In the name of the Father, and of the Son, and of the Holy Spirit. Amen.

Pray the Apostles' Creed on the crucifix of the rosary:
I believe in God, the Father Almighty, Creator of heaven and earth, and in Jesus Christ, his only Son, our Lord, who was conceived by the Holy Spirit, born of the Virgin Mary, suffered under Pontius Pilate, was crucified, died, and was buried. He descended into hell; on the third day he arose from the dead; he ascended into heaven and is seated at the right hand of the Father Almighty; thence he shall come to judge the living and the dead. I believe in the Holy Spirit, the Holy Catholic Church, the communion of saints, the forgiveness of sins, the resurrection of the body, and life everlasting. Amen.

On the first bead, pray an Our Father for the intentions of the pope:
Our Father, who art in heaven, hallowed be thy name. Thy kingdom come; thy will be done on earth as it is in heaven. Give us this day our daily bread and forgive us our trespasses, as we forgive those who trespass against us. And lead us not into temptation but deliver us from evil. Amen.

On the next three beads, pray a Hail Mary on each for faith, hope, and love:
Hail Mary, full of grace, the Lord is with thee. Blessed are thou among women, and blessed is the fruit of thy womb, Jesus. Holy Mary, mother of God, pray for us sinners now, and at the hour of our death. Amen.

Then, pray the Glory Be:
Glory be to the Father and to the Son and to the Holy Spirit, as it was in the beginning, is now, and ever shall be, world without end. Amen.

Then, pray the Fatima prayer:
O my Jesus, forgive us our sins; save us from the fires of hell; lead all souls to heaven, especially those in most need of thy mercy.

For the rest of the rosary beads, pray an Our Father on the large beads, followed by ten Hail Marys, a Glory Be, and the Fatima Prayer. Meditate on the different mysteries of the life of Christ during each decade.

The Joyful Mysteries (Monday and Saturday):
The Annunciation.
The Visitation.
The Birth of Christ.
The Presentation of Jesus to the Temple.
The Finding of the child Jesus in the Temple.

The Sorrowful Mysteries (Tuesday and Friday):
The Agony in the Garden.
The Scourging at the Pillar.
The Crowning of Thorns.
The Carrying of the Cross.
The Crucifixion and Death of Jesus.

The Glorious Mysteries (Wednesday and Sunday):
The Resurrection of Jesus.
The Ascension of Jesus into Heaven.
The Descent of the Holy Spirit upon the Apostles.
The Assumption of Mary's Body into Heaven.
The Crowning of Mary in Heaven.

The Luminous Mysteries (Thursday):
The Baptism of Jesus.
The Wedding Feast at Cana when Jesus Turns Water into Wine.
The Proclamation of the Kingdom by Jesus.
The Transfiguration.
The Last Supper.

At the end of the rosary, pray the Hail, Holy Queen:
Hail, holy queen, Mother of mercy! Our life, our sweetness, and our hope! To thee do we cry, poor banished children of Eve; to thee do we send up our sighs, mourning, and weeping in this valley of tears. Turn, then, most gracious Advocate, thine eyes of mercy toward us; and after this our exile show unto us the blessed fruit of thy womb, Jesus. O clement, O loving, O sweet Virgin Mary.
Pray for us, O holy Mother of God. That we may be made worthy of the promises of Christ.

O God, whose only-begotten Son, by His life, death, and resurrection, has purchased for us the rewards of eternal salvation; grant we beseech Thee, that meditating upon these mysteries of the most holy Rosary of the Blessed Virgin Mary, we may imitate what they contain and obtain what they promise. Through the same Christ our Lord. Amen.

The Chaplet of Divine Mercy:
Open with the following phrase 3 times:
O Blood and Water, which gushed forth from the Heart of Jesus as a fountain of Mercy for us, I trust in You!

Using rosary beads, begin with the Our Father, the Hail Mary, and the Apostles' Creed.
On the large bead before each decade, pray:
Eternal Father, I offer you the body and blood, soul and divinity of your dearly beloved Son, our Lord Jesus Christ, in atonement for our sins and those of the whole world.

On the ten small beads of each decade, pray:
For the sake of his sorrowful Passion, have mercy on us and on the whole world.

After five decades, conclude with:
Holy God, Holy Mighty One, Holy Immortal One, have mercy on us and on the whole world. (3 times)

Prayer to St. Michael the Archangel:
St. Michael the Archangel, defend us in battle. Be our protection against the wickedness and snares of the devil. May God rebuke him, we humbly pray, and do thou, O prince of the heavenly host, by the power of God, cast into hell Satan and all the evil spirits who prowl about the world seeking the ruin of souls. Amen.

How to go to confession:

Prepare by examining your conscience. You can simply reflect on how well you have lived up to the Ten Commandments:

1) I am the Lord your God; you shall have no strange gods before me.
2) You shall not take the name of the Lord your God in vain.
3) Remember to keep holy the Lord's Day.
4) Honor your father and your mother.
5) You shall not kill.
6) You shall not commit adultery.
7) You shall not steal.
8) You shall not bear false witness against your neighbor.
9) You shall not covet your neighbor's wife.
10) You shall not covet your neighbor's goods.

When you enter the confessional, greet the priest by saying, "Bless me, Father, for I have sinned. It has been [amount of time] since my last confession." You may stay behind the privacy screen or sit face-to-face with the priest. Then state your sins and how often they occur.

The priest will give you a penance and invite you to say an act of contrition. You can say your own or use this one:
O my God, I am heartily sorry for having offended you, and I detest all my sins because of your just punishments. But I am sorry most of all because they offend you who are all good and worthy of all my love. I firmly resolve, with the help of your grace, to sin no more and to avoid the near occasions of sin. Amen.

The priest will then give you absolution and send you out into the world by saying "Go in peace."

Parent Page

(Parents, feel free to tear this page out.)

Dear Parents,

Raising pure teens is a tough job, especially in the current culture in which we live. This is undoubtedly one of the most difficult times throughout history to remain pure. Teens will likely encounter pornographic material despite our best attempts to shield them from it. Parental silence on the topic of pornography is no longer an option. Don't give up.

Congratulations. You're holding this book, which is a great way to indirectly evangelize your teens in the midst of the pornographic culture in which they live.

Please place this book in your teen's bathroom after you have read it yourself.

Parents should initiate thousands of short conversations about sexual purity. I recommend searching for casual conversation opportunities when your teen's guard is down. The car is a great place to get started.

You want what is best for your teen. So remember, in the purity fight, they are the victim and the pornographic culture is the villain. One of your greatest assets is the ability to have open conversations with your teen. And open conversations start when the parent is curious, not confrontational. Here are some casual conversation starters to get you started:

- "What are your thoughts on the book I placed in the restroom?"
- "Have you been exposed to pornography? If so, I'm sorry that happened to you and I promise to do a better job of protecting you from pornography in the future."
- "Do any of your friends know about the harms of viewing pornography?"
- "Have any of your friends' parents talked to them about pornography? If so, what did they say? If not, do you think they should? Why?"
- "What would you do if pornography showed up on your computer or Internet device?"
- "What do your teachers say to do if pornography shows up on a school computer?"
- "What are the school's consequences for someone viewing porn at school?"
- "What do you know about the effects of viewing pornography on the brain?"
- "How does porn affect other people besides the person watching it?"
- "Do you think pornography influences our society? Why? Why not?"
- "What does God say about pornography?"
- "Does having purity of our thoughts matter? Why?"
- "What would you say to someone if they asked you how to avoid pornography?"
- "What advice would you give to a friend if they asked you to help them kick their porn habit?"
- "What advice would to give to your future spouse if they struggle with a porn habit?"

For more information visit these fine websites:

PracticalPurity.com
IntegrityRestored.com
CMGparent.org
CovenantEyes.com
FightTheNewDrug.org

Acknowledgments

Kevin and Maggie Anneken

Laura Curran

John J. Garvey III

Jane Hoffman

Nic Kovatch

Mark and Julie Machuga

Joanne Neumann

Mary Lee Olinger

To all those listed and unlisted supporters. This resource would not have been possible without your prayers and financial contributions. Thank you.

To my beautiful wife, Laura, thank you for challenging me to be an authentic man of Christ.

Please pass this book on to someone else and say one *Hail Mary* for all those affected by pornography.

References

A http://abcnews.go.com/Entertainment/WolfFiles/story?id=93103&page=1 (2016)

B Wojtyla, Karol. Love and Responsibility. San Francisco: Ignatius, 1993. 135. Print.

1 http://www.merriam-webster.com/dictionary/pornography (2016).

2 Mary Eberstadt and Mary Ann Layden, "The Social Cost of Pornography: A Statement of Findings and Recommendations" (2010) The Witherspoon Institute, (January 2016)

3 J.Ropelato, "Internet Pornography Statistics," Internet Filter Learning Center, available at http://internet-filter-reviews.toptenreviews.com/internet-pornography-statistics.html. (2016)

4 J.Ropelato, "Internet Pornography Statistics," Internet Filter Learning Center, available at http://internet-filter-reviews.toptenreviews.com/internet-pornography-statistics.html. (2016)

5 Michael Seto, conversation at the first meeting of the International Centre for Missing & Exploited Children's (ICMEC) Gloram Health Coalition, Zurich, Switzerland, October 10, 2012.

6 https://www.theguardian.com/technology/2004/feb/10/usnews.internationalnews (2016)

7 http://www.pornhub.com/cares (2015)

8 Clark, Eric. The Want Makers: Inside the World of Advertising. New York, NY, U.S.A.: Penguin, 1990. Print.

9 http://www.cbsnews.com/news/utah-declares-pornography-public-health-crisis/ (2016)

10 http://www.ccv.org/action-alerts/enforce-obscenity-laws/ (2016)

11 Struthers, William M. Wired for Intimacy: How Pornography Hijacks the Male Brain. Downers Grove, IL: IVP, 2009. 98. Print.

12 Kühn, Simone, and Jürgen Gallinat. "Brain Structure and Functional Connectivity Associated With Pornography Consumption." JAMA Psychiatry 71.7 (2014): n. Web. 28 Mar. 2016.

13 Kühn, Simone, and Jürgen Gallinat. "Brain Structure and Functional Connectivity Associated With Pornography Consumption." JAMA Psychiatry 71.7 (2014): 827. Web. 2016.

14 Struthers, William M. Wired for Intimacy: How Pornography Hijacks the Male Brain. Downers Grove, IL: IVP, 2009. 101-03. Print.

15 After Porn Ends. Dir. Bryce Wagoner. Oxymoron Entertainment, 2012. DVD.

16 Voon, Valerie, Thomas B. Mole, Paula Banca, Laura Porter, Laurel Morris, Simon Mitchell, Tatyana R. Lapa, Ju Karr, Neil A. Harrison, Marc N. Potenza, and Michael Irvine. "Neural Correlates of Sexual Cue Reactivity in Individuals with and without Compulsive Sexual Behaviours." PLoS ONE 9.7 (2014): Web. 16 Apr. 2016.

17 Bergner, Raymond M., and Ana J. Bridges. "The Significance of Heavy Pornography Involvement for Romantic Partners: Research and Clinical Implications." Journal of Sex & Marital Therapy 28.3 (2002): 193+. Web. 28 Apr. 2016.

18 Struthers, William M. Wired for Intimacy: How Pornography Hijacks the Male Brain. Downers Grove, IL: IVP, 2009. 95-96. Print.

19 http://www.yourbrainonporn.com/are-fetishes-innate (2016)

20 Ana Bridges, et al., "Violence Against Women," Sage 16, no. 10 (October 2010): 1065–1085.